# TOMORROW
## *Is A Brand New Day*

# TOMORROW *Is A Brand New Day*

Copyright © 1989 by Resi, Inc.
Published by Harvest House Publishers
Eugene, Oregon 97402

ISBN 0-89081-770-7

Printed in the United States of America.

# TOMORROW
## *Is A Brand New Day*

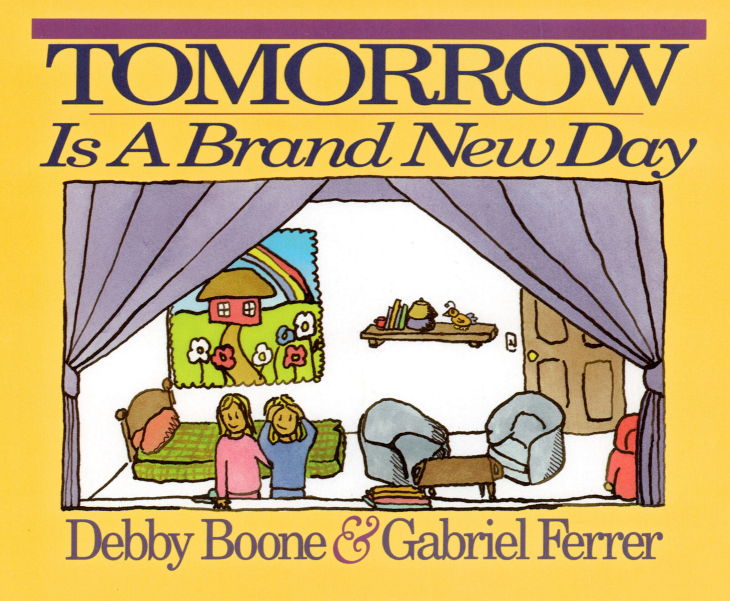

## Debby Boone & Gabriel Ferrer

**HARVEST HOUSE PUBLISHERS**
Eugene, Oregon 97402

# GET OUT OF BED!

Get out of bed **now**! I said out of that bed!
So much to be done! So much to be said!

You can get out head first
or try first with your toes
leave your elbows for last
(see how it goes).

You can jump out or tiptoe
or roll out or crawl.
You can bounce off the ceiling
or bounce off the wall.

But don't loll in bed
though you're warm as a bug.
Just quick! Count to three . . .
and then jump on the rug.

It won't be that painful
not nearly as bad
as a poke in the eye
So get up! You'll be glad!

The whole world is waiting
it's all yours to get . . .
but you're the last one in bed
(or close to it, I bet).

# BRUSH YOUR TEETH

Your teeth need a bath
"A bath?" you might say
Well, not exactly a bath
but close, anyway.

You see, dirt is still dirt
wherever you find it
on the front of your face
or a little behind it.

Your teeth can start looking
a lot less than their best
when they're covered with food
(even food that's been blessed).

So let's get out your toothbrush
(mine happens to be blue)
and squeeze on a big
juicy glop of the goo.

Your teeth will just love it;
you'll see it, here's how:
They'll smile even bigger
Then they can for you now.
And *that's* pretty big . . . but they do it somehow.

## MY FAVORITE SEASON

Of all the seasons that there are
summer is the best by far
barefoot days so warm and bright
catching fireflies in the night.

But then there's spring, I can't forget
when everything's new (and most things are wet)
a time for flowers and Easter fun
Yes, springtime is definitely number one.

But when I think of December's snow
and fireplaces all aglow
the waiting for Santa that seems like forever
I think winter's the best of the best . . . however—

Autumn leaves crunching under my feet
and Halloween candy so yummy and sweet
and Thanksgiving turkey—oh, what a delight
a year without autumn just wouldn't be right.

Why can't I choose? And why should I, I say.
I love the whole year—every month, every day!

# SHADOWPLAY

When there was no one around
when a friend could not be found
I discovered something great:
A shadow makes a fun playmate.

On the ceiling, on the floor
on the lampshade, on the door
you can stick him anywhere
except in the dark (you'll lose him there).

Then there's a game called copycat:
If your shadow does something, you do that.
One problem I've found before you begin
your *shadow*, not you, will always win.

But what I like the best of all
is making animals on the wall—
a rabbit, a dog, a tall giraffe,
or a silly something that makes you laugh.

So if there is no one around
If a friend cannot be found
why not resort to something great?
A shadow is a fun playmate.

# GOOD MORNING AND SMILE

The first thing when you wake up in the morning
and it's time to start a brand new kind of day
why not look into the mirror just a second
and then smile at you as cheerfully you say . . .
GOOD MORNING!

When you're on your way downstairs to eat your breakfast
and your sister calls you a slimy slug named Ray
Don't shout back and lose the happiness inside you
just grin at her and very sweetly say . . .
GOOD MORNING!

When you hop onto that big bright yellow school bus
and the kid you're next to looks the other way
don't get nervous or let yourself get grumpy
just smile at the back side of his head and say . . .
GOOD MORNING!

I hope the point I make has been well taken:
It's *your* choice how you will start out every day.
Don't let grouches take your happy morning from you
Hang on to it—it's yours each time you say . . .
GOOD MORNING!

# SPAGHETTI FOR SUPPER

Spaghetti for supper
what a tempting treat!
Slurping long strings
such a fabulous feat!

You can twirl it or swirl it
or toss it or floss it
or fling it or sling it
Or pour cheese across it.

You can nibble or dribble
without even trying;
you can say, "Mom, great dinner!"
without even lying.

I think we should make it
the law of the land:
Spaghetti for supper
every night . . . now that's grand!

# FLYING KITES

Oh, what a wonderful feeling
what a tremendous delight
you can feel so light, so fresh, so free
when you are outside flying a kite.

You make it with glue and some paper
you tie on a tail at the end
then you get some string (a whole lot of string)
and you find a big place with some friends.

One friend holds the kite very gently
you walk out twenty paces or so
then you hold the string tight and with all of your might
you shout to your friend to let go.

And then you start running and running
and your heart's pounding out of your chest
and the kite slowly, steadily rises—
right about now you are feeling your best.

Then you see your friends shouting and waving
and you know they're as thrilled as can be
but as it turns out what the shouting's about . . .
your kite has been eaten by a tree.

Oh, what a wonderful feeling
so light, so fresh, so free
hold the string tight as you run with your kite
but please . . . don't fly kites near a tree.

## MORNING LIGHT

I love my room in the morning light
before the sun gets really bright
when everything's covered in a soft blue-gray
I love my room at the start of the day.
Light filters in gently as I stretch and yawn
God knew just what I needed when He made the dawn.

## TAKING WALKS

Taking a walk is for having fun—
so much to do, so much to say
you could lose yourself away
when you are taking a walk

Taking a walk is for adventure—
time to look, time to explore
you will see things never seen before
when you are taking a walk

Taking a walk is for finding treasure—
pennies and bugs and bright shiny things
birds to take care of with injured wings
when you are taking a walk

Taking a walk is for feeling free—
free to jump, free to shout
free to let the real you out
you will find beauty all about
when you are taking a walk

# CLOUDS

Do you ever watch clouds?
Watch them come, watch them go
Aren't clouds simply clouds?
Maybe yes, maybe no.

Clouds are all different
though they're made all the same
Clouds are all special—
they each have a name.

There are pirate-ship clouds
with fierce guns and sails;
There are puppydog clouds
that chase kittycat tails.

There are Cumulus cowboys
that ride the sky range,
and Cirrussy clowns
that the Stratus think strange.

So if someone should ask
why your head's in the sky,
you can say, "Sir, I'm watching
that Nimbus float by."

# ANGRY

Have you ever been so angry that
you could jump up and down and chew up a hat
and run 'round in circles and spit at the cat
Have you ever been as angry as that?

Have you ever been so very mad
that everyone around you gets quiet and sad
and when you're finally gone they're all very glad
Have you ever seen yourself that mad?

We all get angry, we've all felt this way
getting mad is not bad, sometimes it's okay
The trick is not staying mad till the middle of May
in fact you should fix it by the end of the day.

Getting angry's one thing, staying angry's another;
resentment that's stuck on the inside can smother.
So whether it's your great-aunt, your sister or brother
talk it out with that person—forgive one another.

And let's all try and live life this way:
Don't stay angry any more than one day.

# THEY ALWAYS COME BACK

When your Dad says goodbye for the office today
or Mom says, "I'm going out. I think to Bombay."
you can be sure of one thing: Though they *do* go away,
your parents will always come back.

Now it's true if you see a red bird in the park
and it suddenly flies when a dog starts to bark
you won't see it again if you sit till it's dark
but your parents will always come back.

Sometimes they'll leave for an hour
sometimes they'll leave for a week
sometimes it seems that they'll never come back
but that's just when you hear a door creak—

And it'll be them rushing through the front door
with kisses and hugs and cuddles galore
and you won't have to worry or fret anymore
'cause your parents will always come back.

# SINGING

Attention, all children! Now hear what I say:
Make sure that you've done enough singing today!

You've heard the old saying 'bout an apple a day
well, singing can help in a different sort of way.

'Cause singing makes you feel really good deep inside,
so good that you'll smile and get all google-eyed

You don't need a piano or need a great voice
all you need is a song (and that's a matter of choice)

Sing songs that are happy, sing songs that are fun
sing songs that you know, (or just write yourself one).

All children the world over: It's my wish and my prayer
that you sing more and more till your songs fill the air!

# WHEN YOU'RE SICK

Getting sick is no fun. I hate it, don't you?
But try as we might, the fact is we all do.

There's no need to worry—so please don't despair
should you happen to catch some bug in the air.

You'll probably be well in a day or two
'specially if your mom takes good care of you.

She'll check out your throat when she makes you say "Ahhh,"
then bring plenty of drinks that you drink through a straw.

Or a bowl full of Jell-O that she'll bring on a tray
(but she'll understand if you push it away).

Or sometimes she'll stand by the edge of your bed
with her soft cool hand on your hot little head.

Why does her touch compare with no other?
Because it's the touch of love from your mother.

## SHOW AND TELL

I love the words "I love you,"
especially from you
but love is not just made of words . . .
it's the little things you do.

Like when you draw me pictures
or make up a silly song
or without my even asking
put your toys where they belong.

When you sneak up from behind me
and hug me by surprise,
or when you play real quietly
so I can exercise.

I love the way you love me
you do it very well.
Did you ever know that loving
is a game of show and tell?

# THE WINNER

"I'm the strongest," "I'm the best,"
"I'm the prettiest," "I'm best dressed,"
"I counted my crayons and I have the most,"
"I'm smarter than anyone," you may boast.

Do you want to cry if you're not the first?
If you're not the winner do you feel like the worst?
We all like the chance to be number one
But you know second or third can still be fun.

It's not just what you look like or how much you own,
If you're first or the best or how tall you've grown
that makes you feel good—really good—through and through
but treating another as you'd like them to treat you.

Some say that to get all the way to the top
you should look out for yourself and don't ever stop.
But I'd like to differ (why, I'll even beg):
Who says that the last one's a rotten egg?

# SUNDAY

There's one day in seven
that stands on its own
and points out the way
to a new week unknown.

A day to look back
and a day you can try
to learn what you can
from the week that's gone by.

A day for your family
a day to just rest
a day to consider
all the ways we've been blessed.

A day to give thanks
and to worship the One
who created us all
and loves us every one.

# I'M THANKFUL

I am thankful for the sun so bright
I am thankful for the moon so white


I am thankful for little bugs
I am thankful for big, big hugs


I am thankful for my family
for peanut butter and for jamly

I am thankful for books I've read
I am thankful for the day ahead

For all the things there are to do
I am thankful for me . . . and you

I am thankful for everyone
I am thankful that I'm done